APR 0 1 2019

Totally AMAZING FACTS ABOUT WEATHER

JACLYN JAYCOX

CAPSTONE PRESS
a capstone imprint

THE ENHANCED FUJITA SCALE MEASURES THE STRENGTH OF TORNADOES.

The weakest tornado is an EF0. The strongest is an EF5.

EF5 TORNADOES HAVE WIND GUSTS OF OVER 200 miles (322 KILOMETERS) PER HOUR.

3

THE DEADLIEST TORNADO ON RECORD HAPPENED IN BANGLADESH IN 1989. IT KILLED 1,300 PEOPLE.

THE WIDEST TORNADO EVER RECORDED WAS **2.6 miles** (4.2 KM) WIDE.

That's more than 45 U.S. football fields wide!

ABOUT 1,200 tornadoes OCCUR IN THE UNITED STATES EACH YEAR.

The U.S. Great Plains region has been called "Tornado Alley."

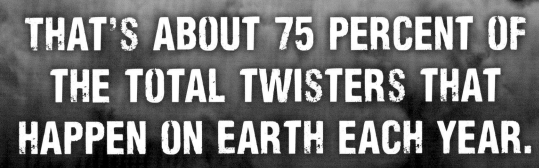

THAT'S ABOUT 75 PERCENT OF THE TOTAL TWISTERS THAT HAPPEN ON EARTH EACH YEAR.

7

SOME PEOPLE SAY TORNADOES SOUND LIKE A MILLION BUMBLEBEES.

OTHERS SAY TORNADOES SOUND LIKE **1,000** JET ENGINES.

9

TORNADOES FORM FROM THUNDERSTORMS CALLED SUPERCELLS.

A tornado can last a **few seconds** or as long as **three hours.**

The strongest tornadoes can toss cars around like toys.

Most tornadoes in the Northern Hemisphere rotate counterclockwise.

Northern Hemisphere

Southern Hemisphere

In the Southern Hemisphere, they rotate clockwise.

TORNADOES HAVE BEEN KNOWN TO BLOW THE FEATHERS OFF OF CHICKENS!

A TORNADO'S FUNNEL CAN TAKE DIFFERENT SHAPES.

Sometimes a funnel looks like an elephant's trunk coming out of a cloud!

13

FLORIDA IS KNOWN AS THE WATERSPOUT CAPITAL OF THE UNITED STATES.

About
500 WATERSPOUTS
occur there each year.

IT ONCE RAINED FROGS IN ENGLAND BECAUSE OF A WATERSPOUT!

In other parts of the world, it has also rained fish, worms, and even alligators!

TSUNAMIS ARE CREATED FROM AN EARTHQUAKE OR VOLCANIC ERUPTION.

WAVES FROM A TSUNAMI CAN TRAVEL **450 miles** (644 KM) PER HOUR!

IN 2004 A HUGE EARTHQUAKE CAUSED A TSUNAMI IN THE INDIAN OCEAN.

It was the deadliest tsunami in history.

It affected **12 COUNTRIES** and killed more than **226,000** people. It also left **MILLIONS** of people homeless.

THE WORD HURRICANE MEANS "GOD OF EVIL."

HURRICANES IN THE NORTHERN HEMISPHERE ROTATE COUNTERCLOCKWISE.

IN THE SOUTHERN HEMISPHERE THEY ROTATE CLOCKWISE.

The "eye" of a hurricane is usually calm. The area surrounding the eye is the most dangerous part!

Eye

HURRICANES IN THE NORTHWEST PACIFIC OCEAN ARE CALLED TYPHOONS.

Cyclones are hurricanes that occur in the South Pacific Ocean and Indian Ocean.

24

THE COSTLIEST HURRICANE IN THE WORLD WAS HURRICANE KATRINA.

THE DAMAGE TOTALED OVER
$100 billion.

HURRICANE IVAN CAUSED A RECORD 127 tornadoes TO SPROUT OVER NINE U.S. STATES.

Nearly **90 PERCENT** of the deaths from hurricanes are a result of flooding, not wind.

A 1979 TROPICAL CYCLONE CALLED TYPHOON TIP WAS THE LARGEST STORM EVER ON EARTH.

IT WAS ALMOST HALF THE SIZE OF THE UNITED STATES!

A LARGE HURRICANE RELEASES THE ENERGY OF 10 ATOMIC BOMBS EVERY SECOND!

30

THE **fastest** WIND SPEED RECORDED ON EARTH HAPPENED IN 1996, DURING A TROPICAL CYCLONE. IT HIT AUSTRALIA WITH WINDS OF **253 miles** (407 KM) PER HOUR.

A HUGE HURRICANE ON JUPITER IS LARGER THAN EARTH.

JUPITER'S HURRICANE

IT HAS BEEN RAGING FOR MORE THAN 300 years!

There are about 16 million thunderstorms on Earth each year.

ROUGHLY 2,000 THUNDERSTORMS CAN BE HAPPENING AT ANY GIVEN MOMENT.

PEOPLE WHO HAVE BEEN HIT BY LIGHTNING HAVE BEEN BLOWN OUT OF THEIR SOCKS AND SHOES!

A PARK RANGER NAMED ROY SULLIVAN WAS STRUCK BY LIGHTNING **seven times!** TWICE IT STARTED HIS HAIR ON FIRE!

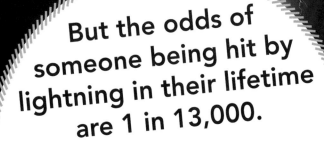

But the odds of someone being hit by lightning in their lifetime are 1 in 13,000.

LIGHTNING STRIKES ABOUT 100 times PER SECOND ON EARTH.

A LIGHTNING BOLT IS FIVE TIMES HOTTER THAN THE SUN!

About 1 out of every
10 LIGHTNING BOLTS
hits ocean rather than land.

IF THERE'S LIGHTNING
WHEN A VOLCANO ERUPTS,
IT'S CALLED A
"DIRTY THUNDERSTORM."

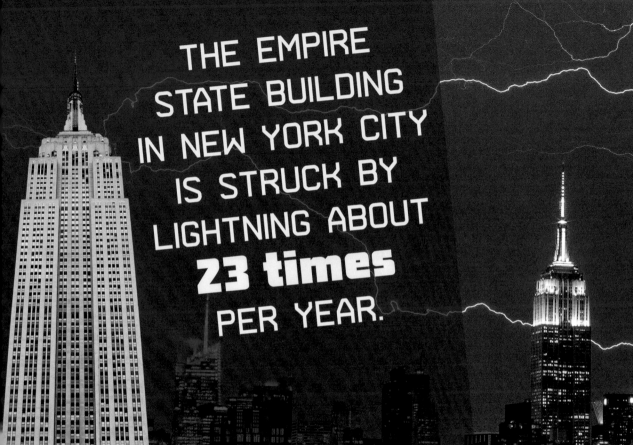

THE EMPIRE STATE BUILDING IN NEW YORK CITY IS STRUCK BY LIGHTNING ABOUT **23 times** PER YEAR.

It was once struck **eight times** in 24 minutes!

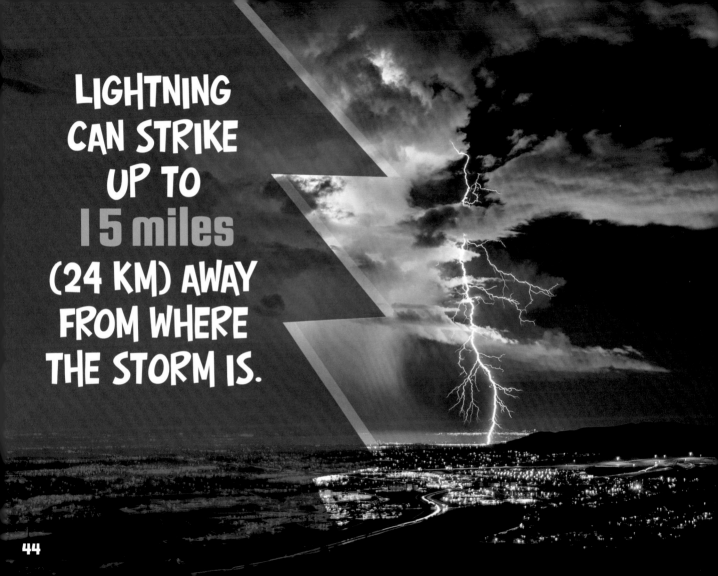

LIGHTNING CAN STRIKE UP TO 15 miles (24 KM) AWAY FROM WHERE THE STORM IS.

A FLASH OF LIGHTNING COULD POWER A 100-WATT LIGHT BULB FOR THREE MONTHS!

A MIX OF WIND AND DIRT CAN CREATE DUST STORMS CALLED "BLACK BLIZZARDS."

A "black blizzard" dropped 12 million tons of soil on Chicago in 1934. That's 4 pounds (1.8 kilograms) for every person in the city!

47

A GIANT WALL OF BLOWING DUST IS CALLED A "HABOOB."

"Dust devils" are like little tornadoes. They are whirlwinds of air and sand. But they are usually harmless.

DUST STORMS IN THE SAHARA
DESERT CAN BLOW A DUST WALL
1 mile (1.6 KM) HIGH!

Raindrops are shaped like hamburger buns when they fall!

THEY CAN FALL AT ABOUT 20 miles (32 KM) PER HOUR.

Raindrops can shoot bits of soil up to **FIVE FEET** (1.5 m) away when they hit the ground!

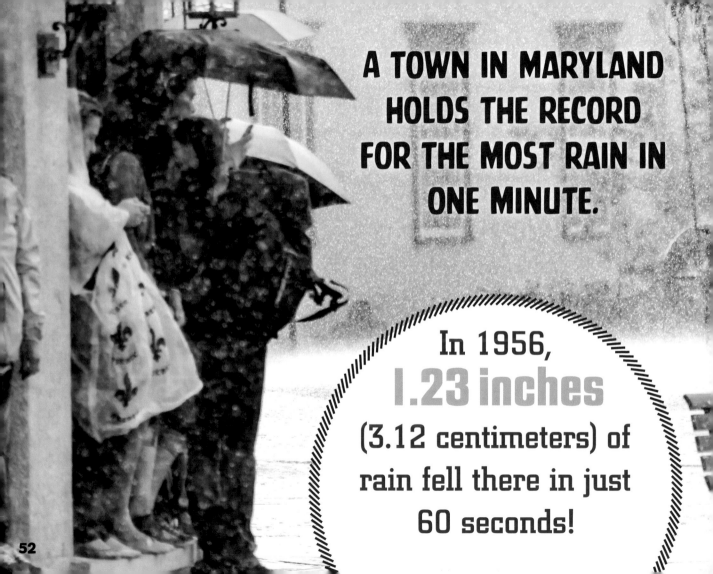

A TOWN IN MARYLAND HOLDS THE RECORD FOR THE MOST RAIN IN ONE MINUTE.

In 1956, **1.23 inches** (3.12 centimeters) of rain fell there in just 60 seconds!

INDIA HOLDS THE RECORD FOR THE MOST RAIN IN ONE YEAR. DURING ONE YEAR, 1,000 INCHES (25.4 M) OF RAIN FELL.

RAIN CAN CARRY DESERT SAND. THE SAND CAN TURN THE RAIN RED.

WHEN THE RAIN FALLS, IT LOOKS LIKE BLOOD.

A mountain in Kauai, Hawaii, is the rainiest place on Earth. It rains up to **350 days** each year!

ARICA, CHILE, ONCE WENT
14 YEARS WITHOUT RAIN!

Lenticular cloud →

IS IT A UFO? NO! IT'S A LENTICULAR CLOUD!

A good-sized thundercloud weighs as much as **10,000 747 jets!**

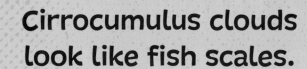

Cirrocumulus clouds look like fish scales.

Altocumulus clouds look like little castles in the sky.

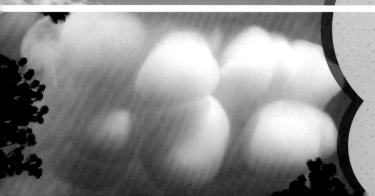

Mammatus clouds hang from the belly of a cloud like a cow's udder.

A FALLING SNOWFLAKE CAN TAKE ONE HOUR TO REACH THE GROUND.

If it lands on water, a snowflake screams! The sound is too high-pitched for the human ear to hear.

Are there really no two snowflakes alike? In 1988 a scientist caught snowflakes from a plane and found two that were identical!

61

JUST 1 inch (2.5 CM) OF RAIN IS EQUAL TO 13 inches (33 CM) OF FLUFFY SNOW.

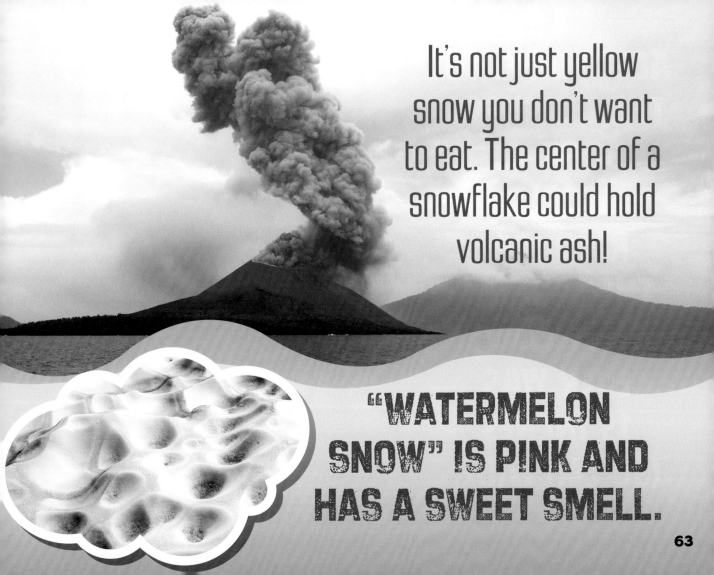

It's not just yellow snow you don't want to eat. The center of a snowflake could hold volcanic ash!

"WATERMELON SNOW" IS PINK AND HAS A SWEET SMELL.

ACCORDING TO THE GUINNESS BOOK OF WORLD RECORDS, THE LARGEST SNOWFLAKE EVER WAS 15 INCHES (38 CM) WIDE.

THE TALLEST SNOWWOMAN IN THE WORLD WAS MADE IN MAINE.

They used **13 MILLION** pounds (5.9 million kg) of snow to build her!

SHE WAS **122 feet** (37 M) TALL. THAT'S TALLER THAN THE HEEL-TO-HEAD HEIGHT OF THE STATUE OF LIBERTY!

WINTER STORMS ALONG THE U.S. EAST COAST ARE KNOWN AS "NOR'EASTERS."

THEY CAN BRING FEET OF SNOW AND HURRICANE-LIKE WINDS.

THE DEADLIEST BLIZZARD HAPPENED IN SOUTHERN IRAN IN 1972.

During that storm, **26 feet** (7.9 m) of snow fell and **4,000** lives were lost.

Two whole
towns had no
survivors.

SYRACUSE, NEW YORK, IS THE SNOWIEST CITY IN THE UNITED STATES.

72

AOMORI CITY, JAPAN, IS THE SNOWIEST PLACE ON EARTH.

An average of **312 INCHES** (792 cm) of snow is dumped on the city each year.

EXTREME ICE STORMS CAN CAUSE AS MUCH DAMAGE AS A TORNADO.

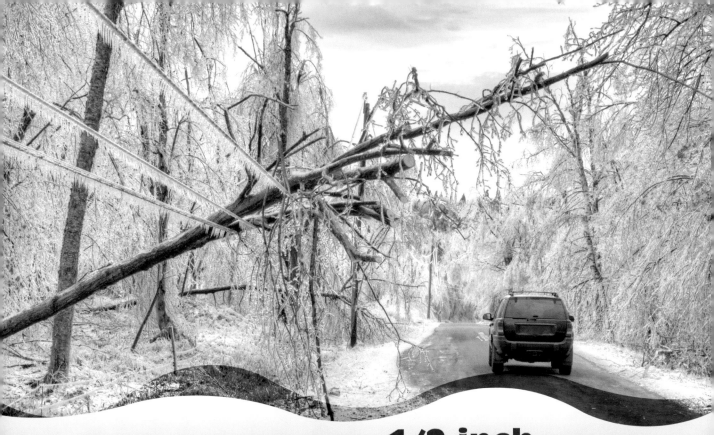

During an ice storm, just **1/2 inch** (1.3 cm) of ice can add **500 pounds** (227 kg) of weight to power lines!

THE LARGEST HAILSTONES ON RECORD WEIGHED **2 pounds** (1 KG).

THEY FELL IN BANGLADESH AND KILLED 92 PEOPLE.

Kericho, Kenya, holds the record for the most hail. It once saw 132 days of hail in one year.

HAILSTONES ZING AROUND INSIDE A THUNDERSTORM LIKE BOUNCY BALLS UNTIL THEY ARE HEAVY ENOUGH TO FALL.

IN THE 1700s PEOPLE FIRED CANNONS INTO CLOUDS TO TRY AND PREVENT HAIL.

CAPE DISAPPOINTMENT IN WASHINGTON IS THE FOGGIEST PLACE IN THE UNITED STATES.

It averages **2,556 hours** of fog every year.

HOW DISAPPOINTING!

AIRPORTS USE HELICOPTERS TO CLEAR FOG.

SOME ANIMALS AND INSECTS
RELY ON FOG FOR WATER.

In some areas of the world, giant nets are used to collect water from fog. It's called fog harvesting.

A HERD OF CARIBOU CAN MAKE THEIR OWN FOG.

YUMA, ARIZONA, IS THE SUNNIEST PLACE ON EARTH.

It receives more than **4,000 hours** of sunshine per year!

COMMONWEALTH BAY, ANTARCTICA, IS ONE OF THE *WINDIEST* PLACES ON EARTH.

Winds of 200 miles (322 km) per hour have been recorded there. That's the same wind speed as an EF5 tornado!

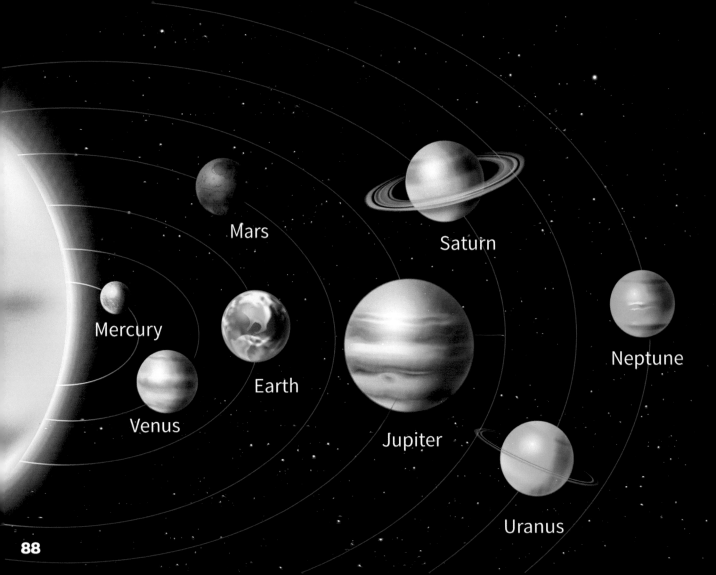

Mars

Saturn

Mercury

Neptune

Earth

Venus

Jupiter

Uranus

NEPTUNE HAS THE STRONGEST WINDS IN THE SOLAR SYSTEM. ITS WINDS HAVE BEEN CLOCKED AT **1,200 miles (1,931 KM) PER HOUR!**

The hottest temperature ever recorded was in Death Valley, California. On July 10, 1913, it reached **134° Fahrenheit** (56.7° Celsius).

THE START OF WINTER FOR THE NORTHERN HEMISPHERE IS IN DECEMBER.

Winter

Summer

Oddly enough, that's also about the time when Earth is closest to the Sun.

The coldest temperature recorded in a populated area reached **-90°F** (-68°C) in Siberia, Russia.

Antarctica had a record-cold temperature of **-135°F** (-92.8°C) in July 1983. If you spit, it would freeze before hitting the ground!

GLOBAL WARMING IS HAVING A WEIRD EFFECT ON OUR CLIMATE.

GAS FROM COWS CONTRIBUTES TO GLOBAL WARMING AND CLIMATE CHANGE.

THE GOLDEN TOAD IS THE FIRST MODERN ANIMAL TO BECOME EXTINCT BECAUSE OF CLIMATE CHANGE.

EARLY TV WEATHER FORECASTERS USED HAND PUPPETS TO REPORT THE WEATHER.

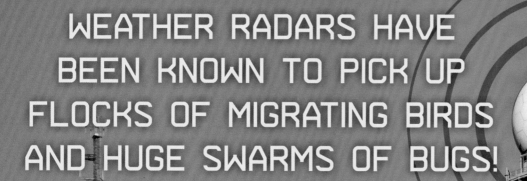

WEATHER RADARS HAVE
BEEN KNOWN TO PICK UP
FLOCKS OF MIGRATING BIRDS
AND HUGE SWARMS OF BUGS!

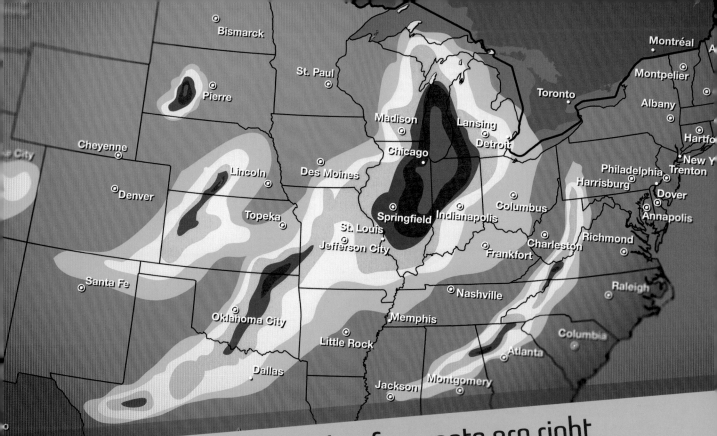

On average, weather forecasts are right **70 to 80 percent** of the time.

When a weather forecast is wrong, it's called a bust.

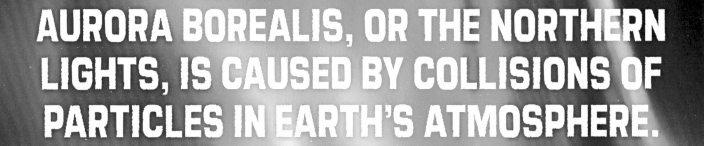

AURORA BOREALIS, OR THE NORTHERN LIGHTS, IS CAUSED BY COLLISIONS OF PARTICLES IN EARTH'S ATMOSPHERE.

IN THE PAST, SOME PEOPLE THOUGHT THE NORTHERN LIGHTS WERE A SIGN THAT SOMETHING HORRIBLE WAS TO COME.

NO TWO PEOPLE EVER SEE THE SAME RAINBOW.

Even your left eye sees it differently than your right eye.

A moonbow is a rare rainbow that appears at night, created by light from the moon.

A SUN DOG LOOKS LIKE A HALO AROUND THE SUN.

Sun dogs can be seen all around the world in any season.

They are
seen most
often in cold
weather
when the
sun is low in
the sky.

109

GLOSSARY

altocumulus cloud—mid-level clouds or patches of clouds that usually appear in clumps

atmosphere—the layer of gases that surrounds some planets, dwarf planets, and moons

cirrocumulus cloud—small, rounded puffs of clouds that appear in rows; they appear in cold weather

forecast—a report of future weather conditions

global warming—the idea that Earth's temperature is slowly rising

hurricane—a strong, swirling wind and rain storm that starts on the ocean; hurricanes are also called typhoons or cyclones

lenticular cloud—smooth, oval or lens-shaped clouds that form high in the sky

mammatus cloud—rounded pouches of clouds that hang from the base of a cloud; they form when cold air sinks

precipitation—water that falls from clouds to Earth's surface; precipitation can be rain, hail, sleet, or snow

radar—a weather tool that sends out microwaves to determine the size, strength, and movement of storms

rotate—to spin around

waterspout—a mass of spinning cloud-filled wind that stretches from a cloud to a body of water; waterspouts force up a strong spray of water in lakes and oceans

READ MORE

Davids, Stacy B. *Strange but True Weather*. Strange But True. Mankato, Minn.: Capstone Press, 2011.

Furgang, Kathy. *Everything Weather*. Washington, D.C.: National Geographic, 2012.

Winchester, Simon. *When the Sky Breaks: Hurricanes, Tornadoes, and the Worst Weather in the World*. New York: Viking/ Published by the Penguin Group, 2017.

INTERNET SITES

Use FactHound to find Internet sites related to this book.

Visit *www.facthound.com*

Just type in 9781515777649 and go.

INDEX

Mind Benders are published by Capstone,
1710 Roe Crest Drive, North Mankato, Minnesota 56003
www.capstonepub.com

Library of Congress Cataloging-in-Publication Data
Library of Congress Cataloging-in-Publication data
is available on the Library of Congress website.
ISBN 978-1-5157-7764-9 (library binding)
ISBN 978-1-5157-7767-0 (eBook PDF)

Photo Credits: Alamy: age fotostock, 103, Phil Crean A, 83 (top right), Philippe Henry/Design Pics Inc, 83 (bottom left); AP Images: AP Images, 70–71, Pat Wellenbach, 66, 67 (snowman); Capstone Publishing: Karon Dubke, 100 (puppet); iStockphoto: -elyn-, 78 (background), ablokhin, 52, Acoll123, 107, Alice_yeo, 42, andersen_oystein, 63 (background), Andrey_As, 7 (clouds), antpkr, 5 (foreground), Astrid860, 60, Ava-Leigh, 58 (background), BABYFRUITY, 16, Bernhard_Staehli, 96 (top left), BradNYC, 42–43, cdwheatley, 39 (background), colebech, 106 (rainbow), crazydiva, 4 (background), CristiNistor, 77, Cylonphoto, 81, DebraMillet, 72, DenisTangneyJr, 75, DNY59, 82–83, donaldyip, 53, Dreef, 68, dwhob, 74, Evgenly1, 35, eyecrave, 4 (foreground), frontpoint, 44, GOLDRAGONFLY, 20–21, Gregory_DUBUS, 76, iwikoz6, 58 (airplane), janrysavy, 7 (background), jerbarber, 38, JoellanaPhotography, 56, Kalistratova, 40–41, Katsapura, 79 (foreground), kevinmwalsh, 69, koto_feja, kraftmen, 3,14, Likoper, 61 (foreground), MCv300, 8 (right), MichalRenee, 63 (foreground), Mlenny, 86–87, mokee81, 100 (background), mrtom-uk, 39 (foreground), NickyBlade, 78 (foreground), Ninja Artist, 34, Nobert Bieberstein, 57, PamelaPeters, 48 (left), Pavliha, 48 (right), photocabin, 98 (cow), Pobytov, cover (background), Pr3t3nd3r, 92 (background), QualityStockShots, 95 (person spitting), RamonBerk, 26 (background), adike, cover (bottom left), Aleksander Karpenko, 94, Ammit Jack, 41 (top right), Anton Brand, 92 (foreground), ArtMari, 29 (background), sasimoto, 62, schnuddel, 9 (top left), SeppFriedhuber, 96 (top right), SpiffyJ, 102, Tigeryan, 20 (top left), TothGaborGyula, 64–65, Tramino, 24, TriggerPhoto, 67 (Statue of Liberty), Warren_Price, 80, yigitdenizozdemir, 26 (foreground); NASA: NASA/JPL, 32 (background), 89; NOAA Photo Library: Commander Richard Behn/NOAA Corps/NOAA Photo Library, 28, Kevin Skow/NOAA Weather in Focus Photo Contest 2015/NOAA Photo Library, 37 (background), Lieutenant Mike Silah/NOAA Corps/NOAA AOC, 23 (background); Science Source: Jeff Lepore, 59 (middle); Shutterstock Images: A3pfamily, 50 (background), adike, cover (bottom left), Aleksander Karpenko, 94, Ammit Jack, 41 (top right), Anton Brand, 92 (foreground), ArtMari, 29 (background), Artspace, 90 (left), Ase, 45, Astarina, 11 (top left), 11 (bottom right), Astrid Gast, 51, BMJ, 99, Bradley Blackburn, 21 (kangaroo), Brian Nolan, 25 (left), browndogstudios, 29 (hurricane), Byelikova Oksana, 41 (bottom right), Caleb Holder, 47 (left), Cammie Czuchnicki, 10 (background), Chris Curtis, 84–85, Christian.dk, 18–19 (foreground), chrupka, 29 (map), Chubarov Alexandr, 17 (plane), Clever Pencil, 96 (snowman), 97 (melted snowman), D Line, 8 (speech bubble), Dan Ross, 5 (background), deepspacedave, 2, Delmas Lehman, 101 (foreground), Design Collection, 27 (speech bubble), Dmitri Ma, 61 (background), Dmitry Natashin, 9 (center), Doroniuk Anastasiia, 18–19 (background), Drew McArthur, 31 (bottom left), encikAn, 90 (right), Everett Historical, 30, Fouaddesigns, 12 (wind gust), gjee, 8 (background), graphicgeoff, 25 (bottom), GraphicsRF, 80 (bottom right), gst, 11 (center), hanakaz, 67 (background), Harvepino, 22 (top), 23 (foreground), Hidayet Mamedov, 11 (bottom right arrow), 11 (top left arrow), 22 (top), 22 (bottom), iamluckylee, 101 (background), Ian Schofield, 15 (top right), ilaembkk, 73, Ira Bagira, 95 (icicles), Jag_cz, 65 (pizza), Jamen Percy, 104–105, JeremyRichards, 54–55, johnfoto18, 50 (hamburger bun), JonahWong, 17 (car), Julien Hautcoeur, 91, Justin Hobson, 7 (tornado), 13 (center), 87, KlaraD, 96 (puddle), lassedesignen, 36 (right), Macrovector, 88, Maksimilian, 46, Martin Haas, 10 (foreground), MaxyM, 47 (right), Memo Angeles, 12 (chicken), meunierd, 15 (bottom left), Miceking, 21 (Australia), Minerva Studio, 6 (background), 13 (left), moj0j0, 47 (background), momente, 9 (bottom right), MPFphotography, 48 (background), 77 (background), 108 (background), 109 (background), MSSA, 27 (waves), mTaira, 18 (foreground), NASA Images, 22 (bottom), 33, nasidastudio, 13 (elephant's trunk), Nateykuru, cover (top left), Nomad_Soul, 36 (bottom), NPeter, 32 (foreground), Orlando Java, 37 (bottom), Paro1, 21 (speech bubble), Pattie Steib, 25 (right), petch one, 6 (foreground), Peter Hermes Furian, 70, Portare fortuna, 92 (speech bubble), Praneet Soontronront, 106 (eyes), Rvector, 55, Sabelskaya, 65 (ice skaters), SanchaiRat, 59 (top), SAYAN MOONGKLANG, cover (top right), Seppo Ryynanen, 108–109, Sergey Krasnoshchokov, cover (bottom right), Sergio Foto, 65 (background), Sherry Saye, 59 (bottom), SIM VA, 12 (speech bubble), Standret, 97 (background), Studio_G, 84 (sun), swa182, 12 (background), Tancha, 17 (cartoon wave), Tatiana Stasenkova, 9 (background), Todd Shoemake, 13 (right), tomashlava, 49, TRONIN ANDREI, 58 (kids), venimo, 8 (dog), Vitoriano Junior, 93, Vladimir Korostyshevskiy, 79 (background), vladwel, 101 (signal), Wenpei, 30–31, XONOVETS, 15 (background), Yes - Royalty Free, 17 (speech bubbles), YevO, 98 (gas), ymphotos, 20 (bottom left), Zacarias Pereira de Mata, 17 (background), Zakharchenko Anna, 27 (girls), zstock, 31 (top left)

Design Elements: Red Line Editorial, Shutterstock Images, and iStockphoto

Printed and bound in Canada.
010811S18